Bookworms Anonymous Cookbooklet

Read, Eat, Meet, Repeat: Excerpts and Recipes
from Everyone's Favorite Book Club

By

Jan Stafford Kellis

BOOKWORMS ANONYMOUS COOKBOOKLET. Copyright (c) 2015 Jan Stafford Kellis. All rights reserved. Printed in the United States of America. No part of this book may be used or reproduced in any manner whatsoever without the express written permission from the author except in the case of brief quotations embodied in critical articles and reviews. For information, address Myrno Moss Perspectives, Post Office Box 536, De Tour Village, MI 49725.

About the Author

Jan Stafford Kellis was born reading and started writing soon after. Through reading, Jan has taught herself how to crochet and machine quilt. Reading gave Jan the confidence to wire her own house and slather Mod Podge on various surfaces in her Craft Cave. Reading helped her master Excel, feng shui and travel planning. Whenever she wants to learn something about anything, she grabs a book or three and educates herself.

She's a wife, mother, grandmother, sister, daughter and friend. She's worked as a grocery store clerk, Tupperware lady, credit union teller, credit union accountant and credit union internal auditor. She is currently working full-time for an electric utility company as a field engineer, meeting cool people and eluding ticks in the best end (not the west end) of Michigan's Upper Peninsula (the UP). The UP provides time for reading (inside in the winter, outside in the summer) and plenty of inspiration for writing. Jan considers reading a sport, and when it's performed outside, it's an extreme sport. If you don't believe this, you've never experienced a UP summer.

Jan is a charter member of Bookworms Anonymous, a reading group established in November 2000. There are a few special things about this reading group: there's no assigned reading, the same seven charter members are still meeting monthly, and there have been two award-winning books written about the group. You can find those books here: www.jankellis.com.

Every Bookworm has heard other readers lament, "I wish I had a book club like yours", so Jan decided to write a Cookbooklet, designed to inspire readers to establish their own Chapter of Bookworms Anonymous.

If, after reading this book, you form your own Chapter, please contact Jan at www.jankellis.com and let her know. You might receive some fun, functional Bookworm swag for your efforts. And of course, you'll be adopted into the Virtual Bookworm Society.

Read on, intrepid Bookworm. Read on.

"Reading is everything. Reading makes me feel like I've accomplished something, learned something, become a better person. Reading makes me smarter. Reading gives me something to talk about later on. Reading is the unbelievably healthy way my attention deficit disorder medicates itself. Reading is escape, and the opposite of escape; it's a way to make contact with reality after a day of making things up, and it's a way of making contact with someone else's imagination after a day that's all too real. Reading is grist. Reading is bliss."

—Nora Ephron

Other books by Jan Stafford Kellis

Bookworms Anonymous, Volumes I and II

 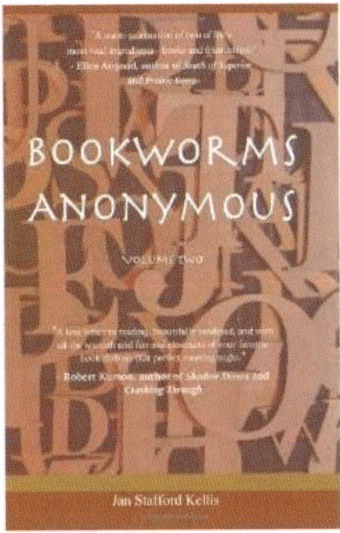

The true tale of a non-traditional book club in De Tour Village, located in Michigan's Upper Peninsula. This book provides a bookworm's eye view of book club meetings (they're never called parties!) and includes book reviews, book handling commandments, recipes and a guide for beginning your own chapter of Bookworms Anonymous.

See the latest news at www.jankellis.com.

A Pocketful of Light

Italy has it all and she's willing to share. Explore the world's original tourist destination through this true story told like a novel. The book features the Fibonacci Sequence, a few non-painful history lessons and some funky Italian phrases as well as the friendly recounting of two travelers exploring the second greatest country in the world.

The Word That You Heard

Enid Forrester hates her name and her hair. On the first day of summer in 1980 she can almost see the wonderfully empty expanse of time stretching before her. Enid comes of age in Michigan's Upper Peninsula, where there isn't much to do in the summer or any other time of year for a twelve-year-old girl. Her summer education includes listening to the "drunken pontificators" lecture in the coffee shop about what not to do as she joins her dad at the local table for their morning refueling. Enid learns life can't be distilled into mere words and small towns sometimes offer the widest view of humanity.

Superior Sacrifices

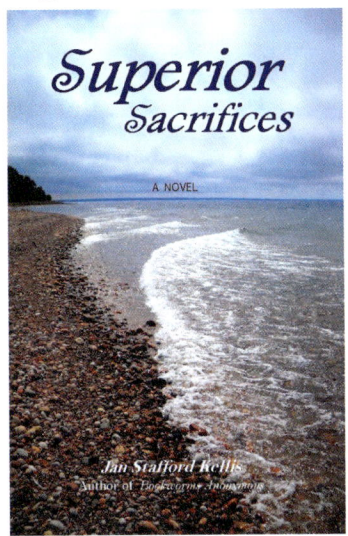

This is the story of Mitch and Marcia: twins, best friends and local celebrities in the small town of Iron Falls, Michigan. Mitch's superhuman dedication to his detective job and Marcia's near-obsessive focus on her family and bookstore business appear ordinary until the secret they've shared for three and a half decades threatens to surface.

All books are available in fine book stores.
For the latest updates, or to book an appearance, please visit www.jankellis.com.

FOREWORD: MENU PLANNING

For me, menu planning for Bookworms Anonymous meetings occurs by whim and fortuitous circumstance. When I see an interesting recipe online or in a magazine, I copy and paste it to my Evernote or take a picture of it with my phone and send it to Evernote. I have a special Evernote notebook called Recipes, and I tag certain recipes with a 'Bookworms' tag if they sound appropriate.

About two weeks before it's my turn to host, I scroll through my Evernote Recipes notebook and select two or three possible recipes. I print them out, then modify them according to the ingredients I have on hand or think I can obtain before the meeting date. I also modify the recipes according to Bookworms protocol: not too spicy, vegetarian (fish is allowed), and it must be on the healthy side. The Bookworms are brave gastronauts, undaunted by experimental dishes.

I further modify the recipes as I prepare them, and I jot down these modifications as I go. I love experimenting with seasonings, so I frequently use the original recipe seasonings as a suggestion and then branch out on my own. I also add ingredients sometimes: if I have extra shredded carrots or cooked lentils, they're probably going to end up as part of the final concoction. When I'm finished, I add all of my notes to my Evernote recipe so I can access it any time, anywhere.

The recipes appearing in this book reflect the modifications I made when I prepared them. Some of the recipes are completely changed, some are only changed about 25%-50%. In making these changes, I've made the recipes my own.

I hope you make them your own, as well. Enjoy!

"I'll read my books and I'll drink coffee and I'll listen to music, and I'll bolt the door."

—JD Salinger

SETTINGS
(Table, that is)

A novel's setting can set the tone for the story, just as the table setting can impact the ambience of your book club meeting (they're *never* called parties!) and ensure everyone is comfortable and relaxed for the discussion. Simple decorations using seasonal flowers, herbs, fruits or vegetables, or book pages, ribbons, beads or twigs can dress up your table and make it more inviting.

Let's look at a few easy ways to add elegance and creativity to your Bookworm meetings.

Don't forget to leave space for a pile of books at each place!

Napkins

We usually use cloth napkins, which are the most versatile when decorating the table. My go-to napkin fold looks like a lily and stands up on the plate. Another simple napkin presentation is to roll the napkin diagonally and tie it with a ribbon, or wrap it with a folded book page.

Plates & Tools

We Bookworms are minimalists, when it comes to things not book-related. For example, doing dishes, even if this means only loading and unloading the dishwasher, is not something easily done while reading. The first law of reading physics is to reduce and/or avoid unnecessary work, which translates to placing only required silverware on the table. The less time spent on chores, the more potential reading time.

So, don't place knives at each place if there's no butter or spread or anything else requiring a knife. In fact, if there's butter or spread, use one knife to serve the butter or spread and let the Worms fend for themselves once they transfer the butter or spread to their plates.

Forks and spoons are generally required for every meal, since some people use spoons for their coffee creamer and/or dessert. A second fork for salad and a third fork for dessert seems like madness to me, but use your own judgment regarding the finished table setting. Add a fork if it looks better or more balanced. And after the meeting, try to wash two utensils at once, or load the dishwasher by the handful to minimize cleaning time and maximize reading time.

Centerpieces

This is where the real creative fun lives. A centerpiece can be tall and skinny, short and squat, long and languorous, elevated on a pedestal or hung from the lighting fixture.

My favorite centerpieces are made from books or book pages. Paper roses, lilies or posies, book page origami dresses, and miniature books are all easy and cheap to make (search Pinterest.com for inspiration and instructions).

Fine China vs. Flea Market Finds

Bookworms revere frugality, without sacrificing quality or presentation. With that in mind, a table featuring various mismatched plates, cups and serving bowls can be a lively and interesting table, possibly more so than one with all matching pieces. Jean once purchased an entire matched set of plates with hand painted fruit on them at a consignment store, and showed them off for us at the first Bookworm meeting following her purchase. I tend to buy fish shaped bowls and platters, so none of them match but their shared theme is enough to tie my table together. I'm not sure what fish have to do with reading (maybe it's their tendency to gather in schools), but for some reason fish-shaped ceramic items appeal to me.

Accessories

Carry your Bookworm theme farther by placing a small gift at each place—a literary puzzle, poem or riddle to launch the meeting. Handmade bookmarks or little book-page figures lend a festive air, as well.

You can find some great ideas by searching online—I have a Pinterest board dedicated to words, and another titled The Bookish Life, where you'll find some great quotes and a few puzzles and riddles. You can find my Pinterest boards here: https://www.pinterest.com/jankellis.

Bookworms, left to right:
Angie, Jen, Jean, Janelle, Christine, Anne, Jan.
(Photo courtesy of George Leonard)

Meeting Format

There's more than one way to run a Bookworms meeting—probably as many ways as there are book clubs. I'll share our method here, and you can modify it as needed to suit your own group.

Most of our meetings begin at 6:00 pm. The Bookworms are a prompt bunch, usually arriving at 5:55 pm. Everyone settles around the table and stows their book bags under their chairs. Wine is poured, news is shared, and dishes are passed (unless this particular meal is served plated).

While we eat, we share our latest news with the group. A few of us don't see each other between meetings, so this is our chance to connect. Not surprisingly, many of our stories revolve around which book we're reading.

As we finish the meal, the hostess pops up and clears the table, replacing our dinner plates with dessert bowls or plates. She serves decaffeinated coffee, refills water and wine glasses, and we enjoy a quick, sweet treat.

The dessert dishes are then whisked away or pushed aside, and the books are hauled out. Each Bookworm is now sitting before an impressive pile of books.

It's finally time to review the books and, more importantly, swap the tomes we hauled to the meeting for new reading material. We generally allow the Bookworm with the tallest stack of books to begin, and we proceed round-robin style from there. It might go something like this:

"Angie, you must have read an entire library's worth! You start," said Christine.

Angie plucked the top book off the stack and stood it up so everyone could view the cover. "This is the best book I've read in a while. I recommend it to everyone." We gazed at the cover of *Mary Coin* by Marisa Silver. "My Kindle games did not get played while I read this book. As you can see from the cover, it's about the itinerant farm worker in the famous photograph taken during the Depression. This photograph appeared on the cover of Life magazine. It was everywhere."

"I remember that photo," said Anne.

"It was *every*where. It's so recognizable, and the struggle she's going through is evident on her face," said Jean.

"The author fictionalized the itinerant worker's life—she calls her Mary Coin—and she also tells the photographer's story, and the story of a present-day person who is connected. It's historical fiction, it's well-done, and it's a good story. I think everyone here will like it."

By this time, Christine had her hand out, so Angie handed the book off and proceeded to the next one.

"This one," said Angie, holding up *The Storied Life of A.J.Fikry* by Gabrielle Zevin, "is a great little read. It's about a single man who lives above his bookstore, and raises a baby who was abandoned in the store."

"I like the quirky characters," said Janelle.

"The setting is what drew me," said Jean. "An island off the East Coast. I love a good East Coast yarn."

"I'll take it," I said, holding out my hand. "I'd like to visit the East Coast with quirky characters."

The meeting runs thus, as we proceed around the table and give each Worm a chance to present the books she's read to the group. Once a book has finished its tour, and has been read by each Bookworm who wants to read it, we donate the book to the gently-used book niche at the Timberdoodle, Janelle's funky little gift store. If all seven of us have read the book, we hold a brief discussion about awarding a Bookworms Anonymous Stamp of Approval. This award requires unanimous approval, and the book is decorated with a sticker and added to my Bookworms Anonymous Stamp of Approval list.

After each Bookworm has presented her books to the group, we schedule the next meeting and place our books back into our book bags. We drive home fast so we can curl up in a comfortable chair and start reading.

Ten Favorite Words
(Too much pressure!)

I've been listening to Anne Lamott's audiobook *Word By Word*. Anne narrates it herself, presenting a portion of her inspiring *Bird By Bird*, about writing and living as a writer and incorporating writing into our daily lives. At first I consumed the audiobook in great gulps, listening at double speed, before I realized I'd better slow down to properly absorb the wisdom.

Near the end of the audio presentation, Anne announces she's going to give us writing assignments to do later. The first assignment is to make a list of my ten favorite words. I immediately pause the audio presentation, eager to attack this assignment while my mind is sharp and elastic and itchy.

Ten favorite words...sounds simple, but how shall I determine which are my favorites? On what basis am I expected to judge these words? I could use words I often use (doesn't this indicate a favoritism of sorts?): fabulous, cinch, scandalous.

I hate questions like this because I'm hardwired to provide the correct answer and when there is no correct answer, I try to read the mind of the person asking the question to discern which answer they're expecting me to give, which is probably an incorrect answer because it won't reflect my style, but theirs.

If someone asks me what my favorite color is, for example, this is what happens:

Okay, I think to myself, *Bob just asked me what my favorite color is. I don't have a favorite color, but that sounds lame. Everyone has a favorite color!* Scanning his clothing and mine, I notice our shirts both have red accents. I grasp at this one similarity and nearly shout with relief, "Red! Yes, red. What's yours?" I'm already thinking if I like red so much, how come I don't have a red car? Red socks? Red shoes? He's going to think I'm lying, and I am — I'm a fraud!

"I don't really have a favorite color," Bob says. Somehow it doesn't sound lame when he says it.

Back to the list of ten favorite words. I'm flummoxed. Ooh! Flummoxed should go on the list! Let's see, it's fun to say, it sounds like what it means, I don't overuse it but I'm comfortable using it, and most people know what it means so it doesn't require translation.

Here's my full list:

1. **Flummoxed** (see reasons above)
2. **Neologism** (I heard it on TV recently, and I'm trying to work it into conversation.)
3. **Bamboozle** (Is this too close in meaning to flummox? Does my listing two words meaning 'mental chaos or confusion' point to a mental illness I'm unaware I have?)
4. **Solstice** (I like the meaning; I like the balance and beauty of the word; it's fun to say, and, as a bonus, it's scientific.)
5. **Malapropism** (I like the meaning, and I like to collect malapropisms. Maybe my next list will be the ten funniest malapropisms I've heard.)
6. **Synergy/Synergistic** (Great meaning, fun to say, not too popular.)
7. **Phooey** (A nod to my grandma, and the only curse word worthy

of a favorite word list.)

8. **Integrity** (An important word; a weighty word; the word by which I choose my friends and those I respect and admire.)

9. **Caliginous** (Shades of the Wizard of Oz; who doesn't watch and wait for opportunities to inject this word into everyday conversation?)

10. **Sagacious** (More scholarly than 'wise', something to which I aspire in my dotage.)

11. (Did you really think I'd stop at 10?) **Flumadiddle** (Pure fun — it means utter nonsense, and comes in handy quite often.)

"Wherever I am, if I've got a book with me, I have a place I can go and feel happy."

—JK Rowling

PROLOGUE:
(Appetizers)

Overheard at the meeting…

"I skip the prologue," said Jean. She flicked her wrist, turning invisible pages in the air.

I gasped. "I'm pretty sure skipping the prologue is in direct violation of our Bylaws."

"It's got to be illegal," said Jen.

"How do you know what happened? Don't you miss out on the pre-story?" Asked Janelle.

"Well, if I think I missed something, I go back and read it after I finish the book," said Jean.

"Only…the book isn't really finished because you skipped the prologue!" I said.

"Sometimes I re-read the prologue, or skim it after I finish the book," said Angie.

"Well, you're gonna want to read this prologue," said Christine, "before you read chapter one."

I couldn't let it go. "It's like you skip the appetizer, eat the meal, eat dessert, then decide you missed something, so you go back and eat the appetizer."

Jean laughed. "I suppose it is like that. Yes." She grinned.

Jen looked at me. "Don't bother writing a prologue. Go straight to chapter one, and make it a flashback if you need to."

"Good idea." I wrote this down. None of my books have prologues. At least, they're not called prologues.

"I don't read the foreword either," said Jean.

"You're killing me, Jean," I said, shaking my head and smiling at her.

"You're a literary rebel," said Janelle.

"I don't have that kind of time, honey." Jean laughed. "At my age," she placed one hand on her chest, "I've learned to simply jump right into the story."

Bookworm Book Handling Commandments

1. Do not dog-ear pages. Always use a bookmark or memorize the page number.

2. Bookmarks must be flat so they don't strain the binding. Index cards work well, as do flat ribbons, traditional bookmarks found in book stores, dollar bills, and small corners torn from magazines. Thick or odd-shaped bookmarks shall not be used.

3. Do not bend the binding backward. This results in a cracked binding and greatly diminishes book life.

4. Protect books from the elements when outside—tuck inside jacket or tote bag to prevent rain, snow, and any other liquid from leaving water marks.

5. Do not read in hazardous conditions, for example, while bathing or bicycling, eating spaghetti or kayaking. Magazines were created for these applications.

6. Carry a book at all times when leaving the house, and always treat books with respect. A book represents someone's ideas, determination and perseverance and deserves, at the very least, respectful handling.

7. It's okay to inhale the scent of the pages. Especially new pages. In fact, it's recommended.

8. Do not write in books, except to note the owner's name. If a particular passage in a book demands notation, use a Post-It note or copy it down in a planner. An exception to this rule is text books, self-help books, diaries, and other types of education books, wherein it is acceptable to highlight and/or write small notes in the margins.

9. When a hardback book has a dust jacket, the jacket must be removed while reading. It's important to remember that a dust jacket is not a bookmark. It was created to prevent dust from accumulating on the book while shelved. Store the dust jacket in a safe place, such as resting atop the books on the bookcase, until finishing the book.

10. When eating or drinking while reading keep the book out of the path of food and liquid by holding the book near the middle of the table, on the far side of the plate.

11. It is allowed, and encouraged, to read while performing certain mindless tasks that won't be compromised by holding a book, such as rocking a baby, waiting on hold, or during the commercials that interrupt a favorite show.

12. None of these rules apply to magazines, which contain time-sensitive material best enjoyed while still fresh, and aren't intended to last as long as books.

Breaking one of the above Commandments incurs serious penalties, including the release of negative energy into the Universe, loss of sleep, and bad book karma.

Fruit & Veggie Wash

Ingredients:

2 Tbsp fresh lemon juice
2 Tbsp baking soda
1 cup vinegar
1 - 3 cups water (depending on size of batch needed)

Mix all ingredients together, and soak fruit and/or veggies for 25-30 minutes. Rinse well.

OR make above mixture with 1 cup of water and put in spray bottle. Spray on fruits and veggies, wait 2 - 5 minutes, then rinse well.

Ever wonder how many bugs and how much dirt is hiding in your fruit and veggies? And what about the bacteria you can't even see? Mix up this wash recipe and soak your fresh fruit in a clear bowl—and try not to gag when you see all the creepy crawlies and the layer of dirt that collects in the bottom! Not only that, your fruits and veggies will stay fresh longer, and taste better.

And don't worry about the vinegar—you won't be able to taste it after rinsing well.

This homemade version of fruit & veggie wash helps remove dirt and bugs, and helps kill bacteria, but it isn't as effective as the all-natural Eat Cleaner product you can buy at www.eatcleaner.com. I'm not affiliated with Eat Cleaner, and I don't make any money through this link. I just know it's a great product, and it's endorsed by Chalene Johnson, so that's good enough for me. If you need motivation or inspiration or just plain good, practical information, you can check out Chalene Johnson here: www.chalenejohnson.com.

Chunky Bean Guac

This recipe is so basic, it's probably illegal to call it a recipe. It's easy and tasty, and healthy—go ahead, eat more dip. It's better than free!

Ingredients:

1 avocado, cubed into 1/4" cubes
1 can Rotel tomatoes and chiles (Hot, if you can handle it!)
1 can black beans, well rinsed and drained

Optional ingredients:

Garlic clove, minced
1 small onion, diced
Cilantro, chopped

Mix everything together—it's okay if it gets slightly mashed—and enjoy on chips, pita bread or crackers.

Sometimes I eat this for dinner with baked pita bread wedges. It's an easy one-handed meal, leaving my other hand free to turn pages.

Colada Smoothie

Ingredients:

1/2 block tofu (I always buy firm, but I suspect any type would do)
1 banana
6 pineapple rings
1/4 cup coconut flakes
3-4 ice cubes

Blend all ingredients together in a blender and enjoy.

Makes one smoothie.

Tofu reduces hot flashes, so drink as often as necessary!

Overheard at the meeting…

"Is that my book?" Jean pointed to the book in Angie's hand. "It has a beautiful cover."

"It's Christine's," said Angie, showing us Christine's lightly penciled initials inside the front cover.

"I think I used to own it." Jean laughed and waved her hand dismissively.

CHAPTER ONE:

BRUNCH

Our March 2015 meeting was an historical event: for the first time, we met at 10:00 am and served brunch. We met at Janelle's, and she made Slow Cooker Brunch Casserole, French Toast Casserole, Healthy Smoothies, Mimosas and real coffee! Until that moment, we'd only sipped decaffeinated coffee at Bookworm meetings because we always meet at 4:00 pm or 6:00 pm.

The Bookworm Brunch was such a hit, we decided to do it again in April 2015.

Host your own Bookworm Brunch with the recipes in this chapter. Enjoy!

Overheard at the meeting...

"I had the most marvelous flu last week," said Jean.

"Oh, you lucky dog." Janelle rolled her eyes. "I've been on the run for the past few weeks, and haven't had much time to read."

Jean put one hand to her chest. "While you were running around, I reclined comfortably on the couch. I was just sick enough that I needed to lie down, but not too sick to read."

"I'm jealous." Jen, Christine, Angie and Anne chorused.

"I'll read your books next," I said. "Maybe there are some residual germs on the pages."

"If you catch it, you catch it. Don't lick the book," said Jen.

Slow Cooker Brunch Casserole

Ingredients:

12 eggs (don't worry, we just heard on the news that cholesterol is no longer worrisome! Go ahead, eat eggs!*)
1/2 cup soy or almond milk
Good-sized handful of mushrooms, diced
6-8 shallots, diced
1/4 cup cheese of your choice, shredded
Coconut oil

Spray the slow cooker well with olive oil or a similar spray, or grease it with coconut oil. Saute the mushrooms and shallots in coconut oil until softened. In a large bowl, whisk together the eggs, milk, salt and pepper. Add the sauteed mushrooms and shallots, and stir until blended.

Pour into slow cooker and cook until eggs are set, approximately 2-3 hours on high, or 4-5 hours on low.

Makes plenty for 6-8 Bookworms.

Janelle served hers with fresh salsa and guacamole, and a couple of flavored hot sauces.

*You may want to confirm this with your cardiologist. Just in case.

Quinoa Breakfast Bars

Ingredients:

1 cup uncooked quinoa
2 tsp cinnamon
1/2 tsp nutmeg
1/4 tsp ground cloves (optional)
1 large apple or 2 small apples, diced (I leave the peel on)
1/2 cup dried cranberries
2 eggs
2 cups vanilla almond milk (also works with soy milk)
1/4 cup maple syrup
1/4 cup raw pecan halves

Preheat the oven to 350 F.

Spray an 8"x8" baking pan with oil (I use avocado oil spray, but any type will do). Stir the spices into the quinoa, then dump into pan and level it out. Sprinkle the diced apple and cranberries on the quinoa. In a small bowl, beat the eggs and combine with the almond milk and maple syrup. Pour this mixture over the fruit and quinoa. Stir carefully, if needed, to evenly distribute everything.

Sprinkle the pecans on top. Bake for one hour or so, until you can only see a little bit of liquid. Allow to cool, then cover and refrigerate.

Makes 9 servings (cut in squares, three rows of three).
Serve the next morning: cut a square, warm it up in the microwave, and plop some vanilla Greek yogurt on top. Dust the yogurt with cinnamon and serve.

French Toast Casserole

Ingredients:

1 (13 oz) loaf white or whole wheat French bread, sliced into 20 pieces
8 eggs
2 cups soy or almond milk
1 tsp vanilla extract
2 tsp cinnamon (or more — I tend to double the cinnamon in a given recipe just for kicks)
1 tsp nutmeg

Optional: Top with roasted pecan halves

The night before:
Spray a 9"x13" cake pan with cooking spray. Arrange bread slices in two rows, slightly overlapping. In a large bowl, combine the eggs, milk, vanilla and cinnamon, whisking until thoroughly mixed. Pour egg mixture over bread, making sure all bread is moist. Cover and refrigerate overnight.

The morning of:
Preheat oven to 350 degrees. Arrange the roasted pecans on the bread, if using. Sprinkle with cinnamon if desired. Bake for 40-45 minutes and serve immediately, with warm Michigan maple syrup for the best experience.

Makes plenty for 8-10 Bookworms.

This casserole is also a perfect Christmas morning treat, so next time you're hosting a breakfast for several people, take it easy and make this exceptional dish. Tastes lovely with coffee.

Cacao Coconut Mini Muffins

Ingredients:

1/2 cup coconut flour
1/4 tsp sea salt
1/4 tsp baking soda
2 eggs
1 banana
1/4 cup maple syrup
1/4 cup coconut sugar
1 Tbsp vanilla extract
1/3 cup coconut oil
2 Tbsp coconut milk or almond milk
1/3 cup raw cacao nibs

Preheat oven to 350 F.

Stir coconut flour, sea salt and baking soda together in your mixer bowl. Start adding wet ingredients and mix well as you go along. Add the cacao nibs last.

Spray each mini muffin cup with baking spray. Using a small scoop, plop some mixture into each mini muffin cup.

Bake for about 20 minutes—keep an eye on them, and take them out when they're beginning to brown.

Makes 20 mini muffins.

These healthy-ish mini muffins are great as a dessert during a brunch meeting, or you can put a bowl of them on the table for a little sweet, guilt-free noshing during any meeting.

Eggs: A Recipe

Did you know you can replace eggs with chia seeds?

Here's the formula: 1 Tablespoon Chia seeds + 3 Tablespoons cold water = 1 egg.

Let the seeds soak for 10-15 minutes, and stir into a recipe in place of an egg.

CHAPTER TWO:

SOUP

Overheard at the meeting…

Angie, holding up a set of three books: "Whose books are these?" Silence around the table. "It's a mystery/suspense trilogy. I know I got it here, you guys."

"They're toothache books. No one wants them," said Janelle.

Angie looked at the cover of the first book. "I read a hundred pages, and-"

"A *hundred* pages? Of a mystery/suspense story?" Jean wrinkled her nose. "Whatever for, dear?"

"They're hot potato books," I said.

Janelle waved the books away. "Quick, drop them back into your bag."

Angie shrugged and stowed the books, lifting another one for us to view. "This one is really good, after the first two hundred pages."

"*Two hundred* pages? What happened to the fifty page rule?" I asked.

"It was the last book on my shelf," said Angie.

"Girl, that is ghastly." Jean shook her head. "But after two hundred pages, the book improved? It was good?"

"Yes, but you have to read the first two hundred pages or it won't make sense."

"I'm not getting involved." Jean dismissed the book with a wave of her hand.

Janelle held out her hand. "I'll take it. It's a pity take, but I'll take it."

"It's a popular book," said Angie.

"We'll watch the movie," Jean and I said together.

Squashed Apple Soup

Ingredients:

1/8 cup coconut oil
1/8 cup butter
1 butternut squash - peeled, seeded, and cut into chunks
1 sweet potato - peeled and cut into chunks
2 large apples — Gala works well — peeled and cut into chunks
1 carrot, peeled and chopped (or, you can cheat and buy shredded carrots!)
1 stalk celery, chopped (if the leaves are still fresh, chop those up too)
1 sweet onion, chopped
2 cloves garlic, minced, or more to taste
4 cups vegetable stock, or as needed
Sea salt and white pepper to taste

Melt coconut oil and butter in a large pot over medium-high heat. Cook and stir butternut squash, sweet potato, apple, carrot, celery, onion, and garlic until lightly browned, about 5 minutes. Pour vegetable stock into apple-squash mixture; bring to a boil. Reduce heat to low, cover, and simmer until tender, about 40 minutes. Puree in a food processor, in small batches, until smooth and creamy. Return pureed soup to pot and season with salt and white pepper.

Makes enough for 6-8 Bookworms.

There's nothing better on an autumn evening.

Yooper Soup

Yooper Soup is perfect for a Bookworms Anonymous chapter meeting, and you can pick two of the main ingredients in the woods or your own back yard, if you happen to live in the UP. If not, you can find the ingredients at your local supermarket.

Best served with tossed salad and a smooth dessert, such as Avocado Chocolate Mousse.

Ingredients:

2 Tbsp butter
1 Tbsp olive oil
1 cup fresh leeks, cleaned and sliced
2 cups fresh Morel mushrooms, cleaned, soaked and halved long-ways
4 1/2 cups vegetable broth
1-2 tsp Sea salt
Several cranks of fresh-ground black pepper
1 loaf hearty bread, sliced thick
6 - 8 slices Swiss cheese
2-3 Tbsp butter

Start the vegetable broth in a pan set to simmer. In a large skillet, sauté the leeks in 2 Tablespoons butter and olive oil for 2-3 minutes, then add Morels. When leeks are translucent and Morels are fragrant, pour the broth into the large skillet and simmer for ten minutes. Add the salt and pepper while simmering.

Preheat the oven to 350 F.

In a deep 9"x13" pan, place 6 - 8 slices of bread (depending on size of bread) and pour the soup over the bread. Top with slices of Swiss cheese, one slice per bread.

Bake, uncovered, at 350 F for 45-60 minutes, until the cheese starts to brown.

Makes 8 servings.

Serve hot and enjoy!

To clean Morel mushrooms: rinse thoroughly, then soak in salt water. Watch for slugs--they will climb out of the mushrooms when the salt reaches them. After soaking for 20-30 minutes, rinse again. At this point, you can dust the mushrooms with flour and freeze on a cookie sheet, then transfer to a bag after they're frozen individually. Or, you can slice them open with the grain of the stem, so you can see the entire inside of the mushroom (again, watch for slugs! Those little suckers hide everywhere) and pat try or drain on a paper towel, then saute in butter and/or olive oil with leeks or garlic. Eat them while hot, or add them to soup.

This soup tastes great warmed up the next day, and the day after that.

De-Beefed Tomato Soup

Ingredients:

2 cups veggie crumbles
1 large onion, diced
2 cloves garlic, minced
6 cups beef or vegetable broth (I use vegetable, but the original recipe called for beef)
26 oz. can petite diced tomatoes
26 oz. can crushed tomatoes
3 tsp Worcestershire sauce
2 Tbsp brown sugar or coconut sugar
1 Tbsp Italian seasoning
1 1/2 cups elbow macaroni
salt and pepper, as desired

In a large sauce pan or soup pot, sauté veggie crumbles, onion and garlic in olive oil. Season with salt and pepper to taste. Cook until onion is translucent, about 5-7 minutes.

Add broth, chopped and crushed tomatoes, Worcestershire, sugar, seasoning, uncooked noodles. Bring to slight boil over medium high heat, stirring occasionally. Reduce heat and simmer for 10 minutes.

Makes enough to serve 8-10 Bookworms, and you'll probably have a little left over for the next day.

Overheard at the meeting…

"Is that my book?" Jean pointed to the book in Janelle's hand. "I think my sister sent it to me."

"It's Jen's," said Janelle, opening the cover to point out Jen's name.

"Jean's?" Jean asked, her hand extended toward the book.

"No, *Jen's*." Janelle grinned at her while the rest of us laughed.

"Hmm. Okay." Jean smiled and shrugged. "It was worth a try."

"I think books are like people, in the sense that they'll turn up in your life when you most need them."

—Emma Thompson

CHAPTER THREE:

SALADS

Overheard at the meeting…

"This one takes place in an old abbey, that becomes a rehab facility." Janelle held up *Rachel's Holiday* by Marian Keyes.

"I guess it's a rehabbey," I said.

"That was so bad, you have to take it now," said Jen.

Janelle handed me the book.

"And this one," she continued, "I bought at a bookstore on our vacation in Florida. A fellow shopper recommended it, and I don't usually follow strangers' recommendations, but I'm glad I did. It's really good!" She held up *The Mountain Between Us*, by Charles Martin. "It's not great literature, but it's a fabulous vacation read."

Janelle dropped the book into Jen's outstretched hand.

"I think I'm the last to read this one." Janelle propped *A Gathering of Finches*, by Jane Kirkpatrick, on her stack.

"Is that my book?" Jean asked.

"No, it's mine," said Christine.

"I thought I brought that one to the group," said Jean.

Janelle flipped to the beginning of the book and read the inscription aloud. "From Mirabelle to Sylvia."

"You stole Syliva's book!" Jen grinned and shook her finger at Jean and Christine.

Quinoa Salad

Ingredients:

1 cup uncooked quinoa (I use red, just for fun. Get it at Trader Joe's and you won't have to pay a premium for it)
1-14oz. can black beans, rinsed and drained
1 sweet red pepper, diced
1/4 cup fresh cilantro, chopped fine
2-3 green onions, diced
1 small zucchini, diced or cut into matchsticks
1 small avocado, diced

Dressing Ingredients:

Juice of 2 small limes or 1 lime and 1 lemon
Sea salt to taste
Freshly ground black pepper to taste
1 garlic clove, minced
1/4 cup fresh cilantro, chopped fine
1/4 cup extra virgin olive oil
1/4 - 1/2 tsp cayenne pepper, if you're brave enough

Prepare quinoa as package directs. While it cooks, prepare all of the veggies and toss them together in a medium-sized bowl. Whisk dressing ingredients together in separate container.

Allow quinoa to cool after cooking, for 5-10 minutes. Mix into veggie mixture and drizzle with dressing.

This salad keeps for 2-3 days if sealed in the fridge.

Serves 6-8 people.

Simple Salad

Ingredients:

2 avocados, chopped
1 small red onion, diced
8-10 cherry or grape tomatoes, halved or quartered
1/3 cup Feta cheese
Slivered almonds, optional

Dressing:
1/4 cup white balsamic vinegar
1/4 cup extra virgin olive oil
Sea salt and white pepper to taste

Prepare the first three ingredients and mix together in a salad bowl. Mix the dressing ingredients together, and drizzle over the salad, stirring to make sure everything is coated. Sprinkle with Feta cheese and slivered almonds, if using, and serve.

Makes 6 small salads, or 4 hearty-sized salads.

This salad looks elegant, tastes great and is easy to assemble at the last minute. Eat the rest the next day as a salad, or add it to pasta (hot or cold) for a lovely lunch.

Dani's Salad

My daughter Dani has a flare for cooking and frequently develops her own recipes from whatever she has on hand. She's also quite handy with a camera, so I'll include one of her photos here.

Ingredients:

1 1/2 cups avocado, chopped
1 1/2 cups sweet corn (frozen or fresh)
1 1/2 cups fresh tomato, chopped
1 Tbsp Soy sauce or Bragg's Liquid Aminos
1/2 cup red onion, minced
2 tsp cumin
2 tsp chili powder
2 tsp fresh squeezed lime juice
Cilantro for garnish (optional)

Mix and enjoy!

"Libraries are the wardrobes of literature."

—George Dyer

CHAPTER FOUR:

SMALL SIDES

Overheard at the meeting…

Book predictions, fortune-teller style:
Holding a book, eyes closed: "I see a trailer…I see poverty…you're reading *A Virtuous Woman* by Kaye Gibbons!"
"Yes!"
(Next book is placed in front of book whisperer.)
"It's heavy. I'm getting a sense of a cataclysmic explosion…drugs and friends and…art? Ooh! You're reading *The Goldfinch* by Donna Tartt!"
"Oh, you're good."
Smiles all around.

World's Easiest Maple Roasted Pecans

Ingredients:

1 cup of pecans (can also use walnuts, almonds or cashews, or mix them up)
2 Tbsp maple syrup

Combine nuts and syrup in a non-stick frying pan on low-medium heat. Cook until syrup caramelizes and nuts are toasted, about ten minutes, stirring constantly. Put on a sheet of parchment paper to cool. If nuts were raw or unsalted, you can sprinkle with coarse salt. Let cool, break apart if necessary and enjoy.

Serve these nuts on salads, stir them into oatmeal, or just pop them into a sandwich bag and enjoy them by the handful. This is so easy, there's no reason to eat naked nuts ever again!

Tomato-Potato-Zucchini-Summer Squash "Casserole"

Ingredients:

1 Tbsp olive oil
1 medium onion
2 garlic cloves
1 medium-sized zucchini
1 medium summer squash
1 large potato
1 large tomato
1 tsp dried thyme
1 tsp fresh rosemary (chopped)
Salt and pepper to taste
1 cup shredded Italian cheese

Preheat the oven to 400 degrees. Finely dice the onion and mince the garlic. Sauté onions in a skillet with olive oil until softened (roughy 5 minutes) then add the garlic until fragrant (about 1-2 minutes).

While the onion and garlic are sautéing, thinly slice the rest of the vegetables. Slice them into the same shape. I used a mandolin but you could also use a food processor or cut by hand (just try to get them to be as close to the same thickness as possible).

Spray the inside of an 8x8 square or round baking dish with non-stick spray. Spread the softened onion and garlic in the bottom of the dish. Place the thinly sliced vegetables in the baking dish vertically, in an alternating pattern. Sprinkle generously with salt, pepper, thyme, and rosemary.

Cover the dish with foil and bake for 30 minutes. Remove the foil, top with cheese and bake for another 15-20 minutes or until the cheese is golden brown.

Makes about 9 servings.

This casserole is pretty. It's festive. You'll hear comments like "I hate to ruin it by cutting it up!" and "This is so good! Can I have the recipe?" and "This is your new signature dish. You'll have to bring it to every single event from now on."

My favorite part of every recipe is tweaking the seasonings. I do this every time I prepare something, even when I've made it before and it turned out fabulous. Why do I mess with perfection? Who knows! This casserole can withstand some serious seasoning tinkering, so have fun with it!

Edamame Hummus

Ingredients:

2 cups shelled edamame
1/3 cup water
3 Tbsp olive oil
2 Tbsp tahini
1 garlic clove
1/2 tsp Kosher salt

If the edamame is frozen, cook according to package directions, then rinse in cool water. Once the edamame is prepared, throw everything in a food processor, and hit go! Spoon into one or two serving bowls and place on table. Can chill in fridge until party time. This hummus lasts for three or four days, so don't let any of it go to waste!

It's green, it's easy, and it pairs well with pita chips. This hummus is also great with the Lentil Packets. And it's so smooth and creamy, you can use it as a sandwich spread. Go ahead, serve it with everything.

Overheard at the meeting…

"Is that my book?" Jean pointed to the book in Anne's hand. "I'll just stick it back in my bag."

"It's Angie's," said Anne, showing us Angie's signature and date on the title page.

"Okay. I have room in my bag, if you don't want to take it home." Jean smiled and waved our laughter away.

"Books are many things: lullabies for the weary, ointment for the wounded, armor for the fearful and nests for those in need of a home."

—Glenda Millard

CHAPTER FIVE:

MAIN DISHES

Overheard at the meeting...

"What are we going to do in ten years, when none of us can remember which book is whose?" I asked.

"We won't remember whether or not we even read a book, let alone who owns it!" Said Jen.

"We'll just purchase 20 or 30 books, and pass them around over and over again." Janelle grinned, looking at each of us in turn. "It'll be the Dementia Book Club. Life will be much easier—we won't have to buy books, and they'll all be good books, so we'll enjoy them every time we read them."

"Maybe we should start a list now, so we can choose the best books for the Dementia Book Club," I said.

"Use the Stamp of Approval list. You know, the best books are on that list," said Jean.

Roasted Portobello Mushrooms with Kale & Garlic

    1/2 cup apple cider vinegar
    2 Tbsp honey
    6 cloves garlic, divided
    3 Tbsp extra-virgin olive oil, divided
    Coarse salt and freshly ground black pepper
    8 stemmed portobello mushrooms
    1 thinly sliced red onion
    Pinch red pepper flakes
    12 cups thinly sliced kale

Combine vinegar, honey, 4 chopped cloves garlic, and 2 Tablespoons olive oil in a bowl. Season with salt and pepper. Arrange mushrooms in a baking dish. Drizzle with vinaigrette, cover, and marinate, turning occasionally, at room temperature for at least 30 minutes (or overnight in the refrigerator).

Meanwhile, heat 1 Tablespoon oil in a large skillet over medium heat. Add onion, 2 thinly sliced cloves garlic, and a pinch red pepper flakes and cook, stirring, until softened, about 5 minutes. Add kale, season with salt, and cook, covered, until bright green and soft, about 4 minutes.

Heat oven to 400 degrees. Roast mushrooms, flipping once, until tender, about 30 minutes. Serve topped with kale.

Serves 8.

These babies look high-class, but they are low-maintenance! Your guests will be impressed with this offering. They look especially high-brow when presented on a white plate with a couple of thinly sliced red pepper pieces arranged on the side.

Mix & Match Quiche

When in doubt, bake a quiche. No matter what you put in it, the finished product looks impressive, tastes great, and keeps for a few days. It takes only a few moments for preparation, you get to warm your house with the oven heat while it bakes, and it smells fabulous.

I cheat by using store-bought crust, the kind in the freezer section, but if you're a pie crust whiz like our Jean and Angie, go ahead and make your own.

Basic Ingredients:

1 pie crust, fresh or frozen
3 eggs
1 cup shredded cheese (Swiss or Italian Blend is best),
seasonings: salt and pepper, herbed pepper, nutmeg

Optional Ingredients (add up to 2.5 cups of whatever you have on hand):

Onion, chopped fine
Mushrooms, diced
Spinach, fresh or frozen (thawed) and chopped
Chopped asparagus
Tomatoes, diced
Garlic, minced
Kale, chopped, rubbed with sea salt, then cooked for about 8 minutes, drained
Sweet peppers, diced
Feta cheese
Leeks, diced

Sauté the optional ingredients, except tomatoes and Feta cheese, for several minutes on medium heat until fragrant and cooked through; if adding frozen spinach, add it last and stir to mix until moisture cooks out. In separate bowl, combine eggs and cheese and seasonings; remove sautéed mixture from heat and stir in egg mixture to combine thoroughly; pour into pie crust.

Bake at 350 F for 35-40 minutes. Top should be golden, just beginning to brown near the edges.

Serves 6-8 Bookworms.

Nutmeg is the silent star here. Be liberal with the nutmeg! I usually mix in about 1 teaspoon of nutmeg, and this is never too much.

Experiment with these ingredients until you're comfortable making quiche. This dish will become your go-to, no-recipe-needed, on-the-spot entertainment favorite.

Spaghetti Squash & Shrimp

Ingredients:

1 med. spaghetti squash (about 3 lbs.)
1-2 Tbsp olive oil
2 cloves garlic, minced or crushed
1/2 lb. shrimp, shelled and cleaned
1 can chopped or diced tomatoes
2 cups mushrooms, sliced
1 onion, diced
1/4 cup diced olives or capers
2-3 cups Watercress or Spinach, chopped
1 cup crumbled Feta
Parmesan cheese, grated, for topping

Heat oven to 375 F.

About an hour before you need to start assembling, or an hour and a half before serving, cut squash lengthwise; bake face down on oiled cookie sheet at 375 F for about 30 minutes or until easily pierced by fork. Cool; scoop out insides.

Turn oven down to 350 F.

Heat oil and sauté garlic. Add shrimp, onion and mushroom. Sauté, stirring occasionally, about 3 minutes. Add tomatoes and watercress or spinach and cook 1 minute longer until vegetables are wilted. Add tomatoes and cheese, and salt and pepper to taste. Arrange squash in bottom of 8"x8" casserole; top with tomato/shrimp mixture and sprinkle with cheeses. Bake for 15 minutes, covered.

Makes 4 generous servings. I usually double this recipe if I'm going to serve it to the Bookworms.

Lentil Packets

Ingredients:

1 cup red lentils (any variety will work; I'm partial to red)
3 cups water
2 Tbsp olive oil
1 medium onion, diced
1 medium potato, peeled and diced or grated
1 large carrot, diced
4 cloves garlic, minced or finely diced
1 bunch parsley, chopped
1 tsp paprika
Sea salt and pepper to taste
1/2 cup of water or so
12 egg roll wrappers

Heat oven to 375 degrees F. Rinse lentils well in a fine-mesh strainer, and put in pan with 3 cups water. Simmer on medium heat for about 20-25 minutes with lid tilted at an angle to allow steam to escape.

Meanwhile, in a large pan, combine the olive oil and diced onion over medium heat. Sauté onions until tender, about 5 minutes. Add potato, carrot, garlic, parsley and spices, and cook another 10 minutes. When lentils are cooked through, add lentils to mixture. Add water if mixture looks too dry.

Spray two cookie sheets with olive oil or other cooking spray. Prepare each packet by scooping a spoonful of mixture into center of egg roll wrapper. Fold into triangular shape as shown in the step-by-step photos below. Seal seams with water. Place packets on cookie sheets and spray with cooking spray. Bake 10 minutes, flip, spray again, and bake another 10 minutes. They should come out golden brown and crispy.

Serve these packets immediately after pulling them from the oven. They taste fantastic with Sriracha sauce, or with Edamame Hummus. I didn't care for the leftovers the day after—the egg roll wrappers became too soggy. Next time I'll try reheating them in the oven on a small pizza pan.

Makes enough packets to serve 7-8 Bookworms.

Step By Step: How to Fold a Lentil Packet

1. Use an ice cream scoop to plop a glop (yes, this is a technical term) into the middle of an egg roll wrapper:

2. Brush water along all four sides with a brush or your fingers:

3. Fold one side into a point like a newspaper hat, as shown below:

4. Flip the pointed side toward you, thus:

5. Fold the other corners over and place packet on cookie sheet.

The Other White Bean Burgers

Chickpeas: the other white beans. Wait—are they peas or beans? And who called them white?

They're not really white, they're beige. Good thing they're good for you, because the thought of eating something beige really isn't all that appetizing.

A friend of a friend once sent her husband to the store with a list containing chickpeas. "If you can't find chickpeas," she told him, "ask a store clerk. Tell them you can make do with garbanzo beans, but you'd prefer chickpeas." Fun with words, culinary style.

Ingredients:

1 can chickpeas (or, in a pinch, use garbanzo beans), drained, rinsed and mashed
1 small Vidalia onion, diced fine
2 carrots, grated
1 garlic clove, minced
1/4 cup chopped cilantro
2-3 Tbsp red wine vinegar or roasted garlic vinegar
2 Tbsp Sriracha sauce
2-3 Tbsp natural peanut butter or almond butter
Sea salt and black pepper to taste
1 cup quick oats
2 Tbsp extra virgin olive oil

Mash the chickpeas, then add everything else and mix well. Form into patties—I usually get 6 patties. Cook them as you would a 'regular' burger (although, this might become your new regular burger!), in a pan on the stove (spray with some oil first) or on the grill outside, or over a campfire.

Double the recipe if needed to feed your whole group. Leftover uncooked patties can be frozen between sheets of waxed paper, in zip lock bags. Leftover cooked patties can be enjoyed the next day or two, after warming in the microwave.

My KitchenAid mixer sports a name tag (Martha) and lives on the counter next to the fridge, where she stands at the ready for so long sometimes she's covered in a layer of fine dust. This recipe is the perfect reason to wipe her down and exercise her motor. Make a double batch and keep your mixer happy!

Tofu Sofrito

Sofrito! Fun to say, fun to cook, delicious to eat.

Sofrito is defined by Dictionary.com as "a Caribbean and Latin American sauce of tomatoes, onions, peppers, garlic, and herbs", but this version has been slightly modified so it includes some garden veggies and herbs.

It tastes like summer.

Ingredients:

2 blocks extra firm tofu
2 tsp chili powder
1 large or 2 small onions, diced
1 clove garlic, minced
2 stalks celery
2 carrots
2 tsp red chili flakes
2 sweet red peppers, finely diced
2 cups sugar snap peas, sliced diagonally into chunks
Olive oil
Sea salt
Black or white pepper
2 vegetable bullion cubes
3 stems of mint, chopped

Heat oven to 425 F. Press the tofu between paper towels, with a plate or other weight on top, to remove some of the liquid. Dice into one-inch cubes. Toss the tofu with about 2 Tablespoons of olive oil, sea salt and pepper and chili powder, and place on baking sheet in oven for 20-25 minutes. Tofu should be golden brown and starting to crisp.

Peel the carrots. Mince one carrot, and cut the other into matchsticks. Do the same with the celery—mince one stalk, and make matchsticks out of the other stalk.

Heat 2 Tablespoons of olive oil in a large pan. Add the onion, garlic, minced carrot and celery, and chili flakes. Cook, stirring occasionally, for about 5 minutes, until very soft. Add the red sweet pepper and cook another 5 minutes, until mixture begins to caramelize. Season with seat salt and pepper and add the remaining vegetables to the pan. Dissolve the vegetable bullion in the appropriate amount of water and add to the vegetables. Stir in about half of the chopped mint and season again with salt and pepper.

Stir the tofu into the sofrito and sprinkle the remaining mint on top to serve.

This dish is great on its own, or it can be served over brown rice or quinoa.

Easily serves 4 as is, or you can stretch it to serve 8 if served over rice or quinoa.

"My two favorite things in life are libraries and bicycles. They both move people forward without wasting anything."

—Peter Golkin

EPILOGUE:

DESSERT

(Photo of Pearl Marquardt, courtesy of Margaret Hubert)

Reading Addiction

My reading addiction is getting out of control. I have 29 tomes in my To-Be-Read stack, and I just ordered Chris Bohjalian's newest release on Amazon.com because I can't wait until I visit the book store next week, at which time I'll walk out with no less than three selections. I already know this because I already know which ones I'm going to buy. This means there's a high potential for purchasing five or six new books.

The stack might topple.

I can't focus my eyes on anything farther away than an arm's length because I've been reading for three hours straight, and I'm pretty sure I can't get out of my chair without assistance because I'm curled into a formerly comfortable posture that has rendered my left arm and right foot completely numb, and I don't think I can bend my ankle back to its intended position. This knowledge lies in the back of my mind—my situation isn't urgent enough or dire enough to tear me away from the printed page just yet.

I haven't eaten yet today; I'm subsisting on coffee and compulsion, unable to look away from the book. If I look away from the book, the characters will go on doing things without me, and it'll just take that much longer for me to find out what they did. If I look away from the book, I might notice the dirty dishes, the dust, the time already passed. I might hear my stomach growl. If I look away from the book, I'll be forced to admit I'm at home in my comfy chair and not walking across England with Harold Fry.

This addiction is a monkey on my back, with sweet, alluring breath that smells like fresh book pages. The monkey carries a book bag, which is the only reason I invited him on my back in the first place. It's a heavy bag and I can't read fast enough to empty it.

And yet, I don't want to read *too* fast. Reading is about slowing down, letting your imagination participate in the story, living alternate lives with the characters and learning trivial facts worthy of repeating at parties.

People should stop writing good books until I can catch up on my reading.

Limoncello Cake

Ingredients:

2 eggs
1 cup vanilla Greek yogurt
1 cup sugar
1/4 cup canola oil
zest of 1 lemon
3 Tbsp Limoncello (or lemon juice)
2 cups flour
1 1/2 tsp baking powder
1/2 tsp baking soda
1/4 tsp salt

Glaze:

1/2 cup powdered sugar
1 1/2 to 2 Tbsp Limoncello or lemon juice (adjust as necessary)
1 tsp lemon zest

Preheat the oven to 350 degrees.

In a large bowl, whisk together the eggs, yogurt, sugar, oil, lemon zest and 3 Tablespoons limoncello or lemon juice. In another bowl, whisk together the flour, baking powder, baking soda and salt. Add the dry ingredients to the wet ingredients, stirring just until incorporated, 15-20 stirs, being careful not to over mix.

Spray an 8.5 x 4.5-inch loaf pan (or alternatively 3 mini loaf pans, 5 3/4 x 3 inch) with cooking spray. Pour the batter into the pan. Bake about 40 minutes for the larger loaf pan or 30-35 minutes for the smaller loaf pans, or until a tester comes out clean and the top of the cake is golden. Cool the cake in the pan for about 5 minutes. Remove from pans and continue cooling on a wire rack.

When the cake is cool, whisk the powdered sugar with 2 Tablespoons limoncello or lemon juice in a small bowl until smooth. Drizzle the glaze over the cake.

You'll have plenty of cake to serve 10-12 Bookworms!

Bring Italy's Amalfi Coast to your dining room with this lemoniest lemony lemonicious dessert. You might want to save a small measure of Limoncello for yourself and your guests' sipping pleasure.

Key Lime Tofu Pudding

Ingredients:

1 package Silken Tofu (Firm works best)
8 oz. low-fat cream cheese or vegan cream cheese
1/2 cup key lime juice or regular lime juice
2 tsp grated lime rind
2 packages Mori-Nu Mates Vanilla Pudding Mix
1 Tbsp honey or sweetener of choice
1 graham cracker pie shell (or crumbs, if making parfaits)

Drain excess water from tofu. Blend tofu with lime juice in a food processor until completely creamy and smooth. Add the remaining ingredients; re-blend until smooth. Pour mixture into a pie shell and chill for 2-3 hours, OR put a spoonful of bread crumbs in the bottom of 6 - 8 parfait dishes, depending on size, and pour mixture into each dish.

This dessert tastes great with fresh raspberries, blueberries and blackberries, and it looks absolutely fantastic with a sprig of mint.

Vanilla Pumpkin Pudding

Ingredients:

3 cups vanilla Greek yogurt
1 cup canned pumpkin puree
1 tsp ground cinnamon
1/4 cup chopped walnuts

Put the first three ingredients in a bowl, folding gently to combine. Spoon into four dessert cups. Top with chopped walnuts, and maybe sprinkle a tiny bit more cinnamon. Enjoy!

Makes enough to serve 8 Bookworms.

It's different, it's healthy, it's orange. You just can't go wrong.

Apple Crustless Pie Delight

Ingredients:

4 Granny Smith apples, diced
2 TbspTbsp sugar
1 tsp cinnamon
1/4 cup granola
1/2 cup to 1 cup vanilla Greek yogurt
1/4 cup chopped pecans

Heat a non-stick frying pan over medium heat. Sauté diced apples until fragrant and starting to soften, 4-5 minutes. Sprinkle with sugar and cinnamon and cook until the sugar liquefies. Divide the apple mixture into 4 dessert bowls. Top with granola, a dollop of yogurt and sprinkle with pecans. Serve immediately.

Serves 8, maybe even 9 or 10, depending on the size of the apples.

What's the most intimidating thing about making apple pie? The crust! We Bookworms are lucky to have two veteran pie crust makers (thank you, Jean and Angie) but for the rest of us, I think we should just skip the crust and remove the floured and rolled anxiety.

Maple-Coconut Fudge

Ingredients:

1/2 cup coconut oil
1/2 cup cocoa powder
1/2 cup almond butter (works best if it's well mixed and at room temperature)
1/4 cup raw honey OR maple cream OR maple syrup
1 tsp vanilla

Melt the coconut oil. Add all ingredients to a food processor and mix well. Spoon into ceramic ramekins or silicon muffin tins, about 1/2" deep. Chill for at least 30 minutes before serving.

Makes 6.

Yes, you can tell yourself you're eating healthy fudge, and you won't be lying. This fudge pairs well with coffee, of course, and it tastes even richer when partnered with red wine.

Overheard at the meeting...

"Is that my book?" Jean pointed to the book in my hand. "It has a beautiful cover."

"I might need an eye exam, but yes, it's yours!" I double-checked Jean's name, printed inside the front cover.

"Oh." Jean leaned toward me, eyes alight. "Did I like it?"

AFTERWORD

Overheard at the meeting...

"Jean highly recommended this book for a sticker," said Angie, holding up a pocket paperback that shall remain untitled to protect the innocuous tome.
"How was it?" Christine asked.
"It was so forgettable, I can hardly remember it," said Angie.
"What kind of sticker did Jean think we should put on it?" I asked.
"Maybe a Chiquita banana sticker." Jen grinned.

Reading A Book On A Summer Evening
...with apologies to Robert Frost...

Whose book this is I think I know.
She left it unattended, though;
She won't know that I've been here,
Grabbing a tome before I go.

This book I carry gives me cheer;
I can live without a library near,
And turn the pages 'til I ache,
The brightest evening of the year.

A book this big, there's no mistake,
Two weeks to read will likely take.
It will not rest upon my heap--
I'll return it when she's not awake.

The book is heavy, dark and deep,
But I have promises to keep,
And pages to read before I sleep,
And pages to read before I sleep.

--Jan Kellis

Reading suggestions

You can find the latest list of Stamp of Approval winners at http://jankellis.com/bookworms/stamp-of-approval/. Print a copy and take it to your local bookstore!

"Books are the plane, the train, and the road. They are the destination and the journey. They are home."

—Anna Quindlen

"A million candles have burned themselves out. Still I read on."

—Edgar Allen Poe

Bookworms Anonymous members:
Left to right: Angie, Anne, Christine, Jan, Jean, Jen, Janelle.
(Photo courtesy of George Leonard)

"This book, when I am dead, will be
A little faint perfume of me.
People who knew me well will say,
She really used to think that way."

—Edna St. Vincent Millay

Made in the USA
Charleston, SC
18 May 2016